THE ILLUSTRATED

ERIC CLAPTON

THE ILLUSTRATED

ERIC CLAPTON

GEOFFREY GIULIANO
BRENDA GIULIANO
and
DEBORAH LYNN BLACK

CHARTWELL
BOOKS, INC.

Published by
CHARTWELL BOOKS. INC.
A division of **BOOK SALES, INC.**
P.O. Box 7100
Edison, New Jersey 08818-7100

ISBN 0-7858-0002-6

Printed and bound in China

CONTENTS

DEDICATION

To His Divine Grace Srila Bhaktivinoda Thakur

"Just as a cloud pours water on a forest fire to extinguish it, so the spiritual master delivers the materially afflicted world by extinguishing the blazing fire of material existence."

From the Sri Guru-astaka by Srila Visvanatha Cakravarti Thakura

CHAPTER ONE

MR DOWNCHILD: THE EARLY YEARS

"I didn't feel I had any identity until the first time I heard blues. It was like a crying of the soul to me. I immediately identified with it. I wasn't sure why I wanted to play it, but I felt completely in tune."

Eric Clapton

Patricia Molly Clapton was just sixteen when she delivered her infant son, Eric Patrick, on 30th March, 1945 in the modest front room of her parents' Surrey terrace house in Ripley. The secret was to be kept for many years of how Eric was the illegitimate child of Pat's wartime romance with married Canadian soldier, Edward Fryer, while he was stationed in England.

In the forties in Britain unmarried mothers were not quickly or easily forgiven, which left the young mother with very limited options. A future with Fryer was not one of the options open to Patricia Clapton in 1945, and so, full of regret, she agreed to allow her son to be adopted by her parents, Rose and Reginald Clapton. "I knew from the moment Eric was born," said Pat, "that there was no way I would have the opportunity to bring him up. The locals were hard on me, but those were the days before the phrase 'love child' was heard of. I shall never get over the guilt, but I suppose that's the penalty I have to live with for having an illegitimate child when I was only sixteen."

As fate would have it, two years later the striking, gregarious young woman fell in love with another Canadian soldier, Frank McDonald. As she prepared to move to Germany with him, she suffered another cruel blow. Frank and his strict Roman Catholic family would not accept Pat's illegitimate child. In great anxiety Patricia had to leave her toddler, Rick (as she called him), in the hands of his doting grandmother. By now Rose Clapton's first husband had died and she had remarried, to a carpenter called Jack Clapp.

Rose remembers her grandson as a shy, exceptionally polite little boy who loved animals and kept a prized collection of snails. At the age of five he began school at the Ripley Church of England Primary School. Eric was an excellent pupil with a gift for art which he appears to have inherited from his mother. When he was still very young, Rose encouraged him to enter a local drawing contest and Eric took first prize, beating some much older children.

Lifelong friend, Guy Pullen, remembers two very distinct sides to Eric:

"He would readily give his toys away. He's always been very loyal and generous, particularly to old mates."

"But he could also bear grudges. Once we had a row. It was his tenth birthday party and he didn't invite me. That's the sort of kid he was. He'd never forgive. He was cunning, a kid who manoeuvered himself in and out of situations. He'd stir up trouble then walk away from it."

When he was nine years old, young Clapton's idyllic world was shattered when his mother returned from Germany with Eric's half brother, Brian, in tow. Although Rose had told him the truth about his mother when he was five, Pat's return affected him badly. His schoolwork deteriorated dramatically and the headmaster intervened. Nevertheless, Eric failed his Eleven Plus exam.

Referring to that difficult period, Clapton recalls, "I was writing my name down as Eric Clapton when I suddenly realized that my so-called parents were Mr. and Mrs Clapp. All the other kids bore the same names as their parents. I was raised by my grandparents under the illusion that they were my parents. My feeling of a lack of identity started then. It explains a lot of my behavior throughout my life. It changed my outlook and my physical appearance so much. Because I still don't know who I am."

His mother, Pat, remarked "It must have been confusing for him when I arrived. He seemed to be very deep, a bit of a loner. I found I'd been kept hush-hush from him which was understandable. He had to be protected from the truth. But it hurt me like mad."

In 1958, when Clapton was thirteen, Buddy Holly, Chuck Berry and Elvis Presley were hitting the British charts and Eric was blown away by this strange new sound rooted in the American blues. All he wanted for his birthday was a guitar.

"The first rock'n'roll I ever saw on TV was Jerry Lee Lewis doing *Great Balls of Fire*. It threw me - it was like seeing someone from outer space. And I wanted to go there. Actually he didn't have a guitarist, but he had a bass player playing a Fender Precision and I said, 'That's a guitar! That's the future.' And that's what I wanted."

Eric persuaded his grandparents to buy him an acoustic Spanish Hoya for £14.00. "Even now in my mind I can see his smile on the way home," grins Rose.

The instrument became an obsession with Clapton, who dutifully practised day and night. "I had to copy to learn. I never had a teacher. I just heard a good song on the radio and the chord changes sounded nice so I picked up the guitar and copied them."

Rose recalls how he would often stay up until the early hours of the morning struggling painstakingly to pick out the chords from blues records with the aid of an old tape recorder. "I remember shouting down to him so many times 'Rick, your father's got to go to work in the morning!'"

With this new preoccupation Eric retreated further into himself. The shy boy was now becoming the teenage loner to the people of Ripley. "He had the tightest jeans, the longest hair, a dirty face and he would sit alone on the village green playing this guitar to himself," recalls Pullen. "Oh yeah, he was certainly the odd one out."

Adds Rose, "If another boy came up to him as he was sitting on the green Rick would say, 'Hey listen to this blues guitar.' He'd try to emulate the blues sound and the blues notes every day throughout the summer."

In return for the Clapps' purchase of his guitar, Eric agreed to carry on with his studies and attend Hollyfield Road School in Surbiton, before entering the Kingston School of Art two years later. Britain's art schools are among its best educational establishments and they have certainly produced many great rock musicians - Pete Townshend, Keith Richards and Ray Davies, to name but a few.

"I didn't have enough certificates, but I took a portfolio and they liked what they saw. I got into the art school for one year on probation. I told them I wanted to be a commercial artist so they put me into graphic design. After the first couple of weeks I realized I was in the wrong department because in the canteen I saw all the blokes with paint all over them and long hair. They were in the Fine Arts Department. I really thought I'd blown it from the word go."

A conflict soon developed between art and music, however, and the latter won. Clapton would take his guitar to school, where he quickly gained popularity for his lunchtime performances in the cafeteria. He soon began skipping classes and spent his time looking for rare imports in local record shops or practising guitar. Inevitably letters from the principal began arriving at the Clapp home.

Of his dismissal from art school Eric admitted, "I was shocked. What I was doing was creative and imaginative. Simply because of a lot of distractions, getting into the bohemian, beatnik thing and listening to music I didn't have a big enough portfolio. They booted me out with one other bloke - only two of us out of fifty, which wasn't too good."

Eric's grandfather then took him on as a bricklayer and found he had a flair for laying tiles. Surprizingly this practical task had a profound effect on Clapton: "By watching him and his dexterity and skill I realized that little things are all-important. It was magic to watch him work. He could plaster a room in two hours and it was phenomenal, a work of art."

Off the job, nights were spent plunging into the Kingston beatnik scene, frequenting haunts such as the Crown pub, L'Auberge coffee bar and the blues club on nearby Eel Pie Island. By 1962 Clapton had totally immersed himself in the bohemian lifestyle, emulating guitar heroes Brownie McGhee, Robert Johnson and Big Bill Broonzy.

Eventually he abandoned his day job and took up a hobo-like existence, sleeping on park benches or crashing on friends' floors. He hooked up with blues guitarist, Dave Brock, and the two of them landed gigs at various Kingston and Richmond folk clubs and coffee bars.

It was early in 1963 though, when Clapton got his first big break. An art college friend introduced him to Tom McGuinness, and together with drummer Robin Mason, pianist Ben Palmer and vocalist Terry Brennan they formed a blues group called The Roosters, after the Willie Dixon song *Little Red Rooster*, with which the Rolling Stones were to have a big hit at the end of 1964.

"He had a fluency and command that seemed endless," Palmer immediately noticed. "He had a sense of dynamics quite remarkable for someone his age. He was so good, obviously a natural. He joined the band then and there."

"I knew from the very first he was different from the rest of us, the telling factor was that he didn't mind taking solos. He'd go on and on until sometimes you'd have to stop him to bring the singer back in. He was lucid, fresh, powerful, always building."

Clapton remembers those days as amongst the best of his life, living in an artists' commune with Palmer above a warehouse in Covent Garden, drinking cheap Algerian red wine and playing for a few pounds a night. And yet he could always come back home. "My grandparents were very fun-loving people and I was always happy to take people back there. I'd go to London and hang out with these bums and wandering troubadours who'd go back to Ripley with me and meet my grandparents. My grandparents remember them all to this day."

Clapton's musical growth and development soon created a professional friction with Palmer. Eric found the blues purist too restrictive for his own eager exploration of other musical influences. After six months they agreed to an amicable split, still remaining the best of friends.

Eric and Tom McGuinness joined another band called Casey and The Engineers. Their stodgy Liverpool pop sound was, however, unpalatable to Eric and he quit after just six weeks. His whole life was about to change though. The skinny eighteen-year-old guitar wizard was about to go electric and take his first tentative steps towards stardom.

CHAPTER TWO

MONEY AND CIGARETTES: THE YARDBIRDS AND JOHN MAYALL

"I took everything far too seriously. It's a strength, yeah, but it can also be a hell of a stumbling block in terms of relationships, like getting on with other musicians. Perhaps if I'd been able to temper things, I'd have been a happier person."

Eric Clapton

One Sunday evening in October of 1963 Eric went to the Crawdaddy Club at the Station Hotel in Richmond to hear a new band led by vocalist Keith Relf, a friend from Kingston Art School. The newly-formed five-piece, The Yardbirds, had taken over the regular Sunday evening spot at the Crawdaddy Club from the Rolling Stones, who had just secured their record deal with Decca.

Clapton liked what he heard, a rough-edged contemporary blend of R&B in the style of Bo Diddley and Jimmy Reed. It just so happened that the group's guitarist, 'Top' Topham, was leaving and Eric was promptly offered the position which he accepted on the spot. The line-up was now Keith Relf (vocals), Paul Samwell-Smith (bass), Chris Dreja (guitar), Jim McCarty (drums) and, of course, Eric on lead guitar.

It was then that Clapton acquired his first electric guitar, a massive Ray double cutaway - "a bitch to play" according to him. His grandparents bought the instrument on an instalment plan, but Rose warned him, "You're wasting your time on that thing. It's a nice hobby but not really a job. If that's what you want to do, okay, but don't blame us if things go wrong."

"It won't go wrong Mum, don't worry," he promised.

Clapton soon found himself earning £20.00 a week playing the Crawdaddy and Studio 51 under the management of promoter Giorgio Gomelsky, noted for coining Eric's famous nickname, 'Slowhand.' "He coined it as a good pun," Clapton explained. "He kept saying I was a fast player, so he put together the slow-handclap phrase into 'Slowhand' as a play on words."

It didn't take long for the young guitarist to gain a considerable reputation. Crowds would gather at his side of the stage, mesmerized by his

The Yardbirds in Hyde Park, London, in April, 1964.

uncanny command of his instrument. Paul Samwell-Smith, the band's bass player, remembers, "He was certainly the best musician in the band, by far the most lucid. He'd move to the front of the stage and take a solo and we'd all know it was something special."

Clapton was ever conscious of his bluesman image, right down to his wardrobe. While the other Yardbirds wore jeans and denim jackets, Eric was to be seen in sharp suits, Italian shoes and a neat, short haircut. "I always fancied myself as being part of an elite. A blues guitar player was almost like being a jazz musician. I loved the idea that jazz musicians were very slick looking guys. And that was for me. I was mad about clothes. I could have been a fashion designer because I've always been fascinated by clothes."

Another perk of fame was the sudden overwhelming attention of women. "I think I've slept with about a thousand girls," he admitted years later. "It was a childhood ambition. I thought I'd missed out because I didn't know about the facts of life until I was nine and I thought everyone else had known about them since they came out of the womb."

In fact, he was acting out the first of several addictive behavior patterns motivated by a deep-seated inner turmoil that would reach a crisis point many years later.

By February, 1964, The Yardbirds were flying high, having secured not only a regular gig at the trendy Marquee Club in London, but also a record contract with EMI. Following their first single, Billy Boy Arnold's *I Wish You Would*, released in June, the band began a gruelling six month tour of Scotland and England, which included The Beatles' famous haunt, Liverpool's Cavern Club.

It was The Yardbirds' second release, Sonny Boy Williamson's *Good Morning Little Schoolgirl*, that propelled the group into the spotlight. (In 1965 they were rated third in popularity among music fans behind The Beatles and The Rolling Stones). The song featured Eric's first recorded vocal and initial evidence of his violin-like sustain on guitar. "That was a bit risky," he later admitted, "because it wasn't part of the blues tradition to have feedback guitar. I wanted my guitar to sound like a shanha, an Indian reed instrument which has a long sustain."

Clapton's growing technical ability didn't impress all his peers, however, notably The Who's Pete Townshend: "I had no time for hybrid white blues. To me, a London white performer trying to play blues music was a joke. The Who at least turned it into slightly more of our own urban form of music that depended very much on the lyrics. How could a young white boy from Surrey hope to sing or play the blues?" The pair's initial meeting occurred at a London bus stop, with Eric exhibiting the natural arrogance that had first emerged in childhood. "Although he was charming," admitted Townshend, "he didn't treat me as if there was any substance to me. It was a bit of a one-sided affair. Musically he felt superior and I certainly did."

It was during his stint with The Yardbirds that Eric visited Germany for his first adult contact with Patricia, an awkward experience that opened

The Yardbirds.
Left to right: Chris Dreja, Eric Clapton, Paul Smith, Jim McCarty and Keith Relf.

old wounds for both mother and son. Pat confessed, "We still couldn't talk about being mother and son. He looked at me, I looked at him; the knowledge was there but we both found it too painful." Eric agreed to refer to Pat as his sister whenever they were in company. "It saved us explaining the tangled web of relationships," she said. "As the years went by Rick told me that when he realized he was illegitimate that was one of the reasons he had to make a name for himself. To overcome his background and strive for something."

By 1965 there were serious personality problems within The Yardbirds. Eric's relationship with Samwell-Smith, on shaky ground right from the start, deteriorated badly when manager, Giorgio Gomelsky, made Paul the official band leader. "He had such a tweedy image," complained Clapton. "He lived with his mum and dad and it was all so perfectly normal. He was such a good boy! I was into hanging out with people who were more likely to be rebels, from broken homes and generally neurotic."

Samwell-Smith countered: "Eric regarded me as a snob who was jumping on the blues bandwagon, who had no right to lead the group. Our manager told him he must do exactly as I said. That didn't go down well at all."

In addition to these personality problems, on the musical front The Yardbirds were becoming far too commercial for Eric's taste. The breaking point came early in 1965 with the recording of their number three single, *For Your Love*, a piece which Clapton despised for its tacky harpsichord and bongo-drum backing. On top of that, the B-side, *Got To Hurry*, Clapton's first attempt at composing was credited to Gomelsky under the pseudonym 'Rasputin'.

An early ad for The Yardbirds.

"The atmosphere was a political thrust towards the top of the charts," remembers Eric. "It didn't appeal to me to end up on television and do cabaret and package tours. The more ambitious they got for the money, the less happy I became. Money never meant anything to me because I've always been a bit of a scrounger. I wanted out."

As the headlines in March, 1965 cried, "Clapton Quits Yardbirds - Too Commercial" Eric dropped out of the public eye for several months, practising incessantly and immersing himself instead in the gritty, primal music of Delta blues giant Robert Johnson, who was murdered in 1938.

Then in April of 1965 Clapton received a call from the great British

The Yardbirds on the Serpentine lake in London's Hyde Park in 1964.

blues guitarist, John Mayall, offering him a position in his respected R&B band, The Bluesbreakers. Twelve years Clapton's senior, Mayall cut a commanding presence and the two shared an instant rapport. John brought the twenty-year-old into his home, where together they listened to and discussed Mayall's enormous collection of blues records. "He listened to me about music, one of the few people who did," remembers Clapton. "He was easy company, keen to draw me out and find out what I thought. I did flower a lot during my time with Mayall."

Assessing Clapton's talent, John has said, "When he was with The Yardbirds he wasn't that remarkable, but obviously he was the one you'd look for in the group if you were a blues lover. It's remarkable how quickly he progressed in The Bluesbreakers because he put a lot of time in getting his foundations right. There's never been a guitar player like Eric as regards blues and in my opinion there never will be. When he felt like playing a slow blues he could send shivers down your spine. He was a one-off."

Clapton's year-long tenure with the band featured blues by the book on his prized Gibson Les Paul. In the studio he insisted on playing through big Marshall amps at full volume, which produced a sustained power tone as explosive as anything he's ever recorded.

When Rose Clapp first heard Clapton playing with The Bluesbreakers, she said, "It brought a lump to my throat. I used to say to Jack, 'There's something inside that boy that's got to come out somewhere.' Now when

Right: Yardbird Clapton in repose.

Above: An early endorsement by Clapton for
Sound City strings.

BLUES BREAKERS JOHN MAYALL WITH ERIC CLAPTON

DERAM
800 086-2

he got going with John Mayall I got to see that maybe that shyness in him as a young boy was just waiting to come through in this way. Of course he calls it the blues, but I reckon it's something he's invented."

Eric's growing popularity became clear as fans began flocking to Bluesbreakers concerts solely to see the sizzling guitarman. They chanted "Clapton is God!" and the slogan began to appear regularly on the walls of London tube stations and in the toilets of R&B clubs. "My vanity was incredibly boosted by the God thing," he later admitted. "I got this false self-confidence and then I realized I was talking so much rubbish to everyone around me. So I withdrew and became an introvert."

Clapton's pre-eminence in the band was demonstrated on the groundbreaking top ten album entitled *John Mayall's Bluesbreakers* featuring Eric Clapton. The album was especially memorable for Eric's first lead vocal, singing on Robert Johnson's *Rambling On My Mind*.

By spring of 1966, however, Mayall began observing a restlessness in his young star and a growing need to move on. Eric later said, "I was feeding on a lot of other directions and I started to look at the whole Mayall thing as a dead-end street. I just wanted to get further than the band was going which was in the Chicago blues field. I wanted to go somewhere else."

That somewhere would, of course, be the highest level of rock success and an unchallenged position in the blues hierarchy.

CHAPTER THREE

STRANGE BREW: CREAM

"I got really hung up. I tried to write pure pop songs and create a pop image. It was a sham, because I wasn't being true to myself. I became a rock star. Even though it was against my will to begin with, that's the way it turned out."

Eric Clapton

In Oxford, during one of his final gigs with Mayall, Clapton was ligging about during the interval when he turned to see drummer Ginger Baker. Familiar with Baker's sterling work with people such as Alexis Korner and Graham Bond, he eagerly offered, "Hey Ginge, we gotta have a play."

Sparks immediately flew as the two brilliant musicians got everyone in the crowd on their feet, begging for more. It proved to be more than an impromptu jam; Baker was there to offer Eric a place in the new band he was getting together.

"Sure, I'm there," Eric replied, "but we'd have to have Jack Bruce as well." Familiar with the Scottish bassist from his brief, but impressive stints in Mayall's Bluesbreakers, Clapton felt that Bruce was the ideal choice.

It was a condition which Baker hadn't anticipated. Just six months earlier he had personally fired the talented 23-year-old Bruce from The Graham Bond Organization (at knife point Bruce claimed). Ginger and Jack had a history of being a formidable, highly charged rhythm section whose personal and professional clashes sometimes caused them literally to come to blows, even on stage. Finally Baker admitted that, "Jack is the best bass player around," and Bruce decided to leave Manfred Mann to become the third member of the trio.

Assembling at Baker's Neasden home for their first rehearsal, no-one quite knew what to expect. But as soon as the three-some launched into blues classics such as *Hey Lawdy Mamma* and *Catsquirrel*, something extraordinary happened. The three produced a sound so dynamic that the local kids began to gather outside, dancing to this remarkable new sound described by Baker as "pure instanta-

Above and opposite: The boys in the band when things were still good.

Opposite, above and overleaf: Cream on British TV's "Ready, Steady, Go" in 1966.

neous magic."

In that heady moment of exhilaration Eric blurted out, "Yeah man, we're the cream!" and the first ever 'supergroup' was officially born.

Clapton later admitted harboring a fantasy that never quite came to pass. "I would be the slick front man, the Buddy Guy type with the big suit, baggy trousers, doing straight blues. The other two would be the perfect backup. When we had our first rehearsal that just went complete-ly out the window and they took over. Jack brought in songs he'd written and I just had to go along with it. I let my idea take a back seat and actually die in the end."

Under the careful management of showbiz impresario, Robert Stigwood, the new band made an immediate nationwide impact. On the strength of Clapton's reputation, the trio's debut on 2nd July, 1966, at the Twisted Wheel in Manchester, drew a packed house.

Signs of 'Clapton Is God' took Baker by surprise. "I wasn't really aware of his huge following. To me he was just a very young, gifted player and a hell of a sweet guy. But when I saw 'Clapton Is God' on the walls, it was quite a revelation."

At Cream's second appearance at the annual National Jazz and Blues Festival held in Windsor, despite the rain-soaked conditions, an ecstatic crowd of 10,000 wildly cheered this adventurous trio which had laid a

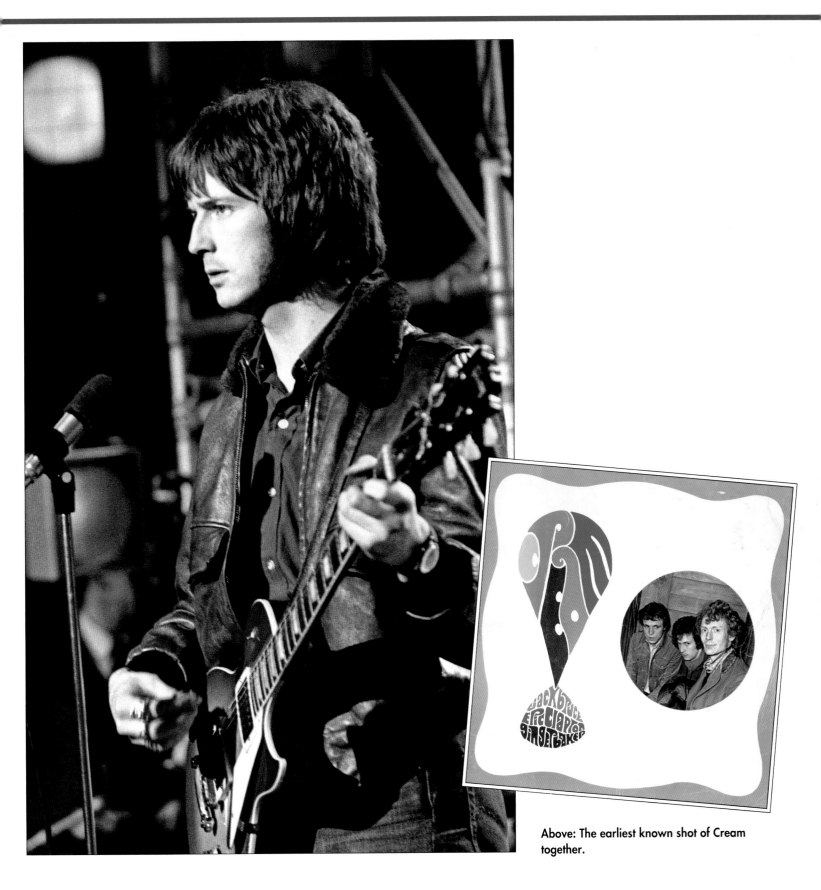

Above: The earliest known shot of Cream together.

blues/jazz fusion over a foundation that was solid rock.

"What made us different from any other band," recalls Bruce, "was that Ginger had a rhythm element, Eric had a knowledge of the blues and I had something else, my own statement, that took the band in a whole new direction."

Overleaf: Bruce, Baker and Clapton hanging out with a friend.

Opposite top: An early shot of Cream.

Right: Cream at a later stage in their meteoric career.

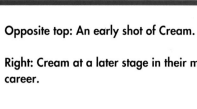

Opposite centre: An early, glowing review.

Opposite below: Baker in his early days on the jazz circuit in London.

Eric Clapton

Ginger Baker

Jack Bruce

HULL LAPPED UP CREAM

THE CREAM — the dynamic new product on the British pop market —poured out a sample of their sensational sound in the Skyline Ballroom this week . . . and Hull lapped it up.

The group belted out a bluesy approach to pop music, filling the dance room with an electric atmosphere—and the result was one of the best dances Hull has seen for a long time.

If talent has anything to do with it, The Cream are destined for a bright future, and it is not surprising, for the group consists of three of the country's top pop - blues musicians.

Their music is exciting, quietly commercial and refreshingly original. It is alive, skilfully played and compelling.

The teenagers were stunned. Of course, the Cream's reputation grows every day, but no one expected them to be as good as they turned out to be.

Reverence

A large interested crowd gathered round the stage and treated the group with a strange sort of reverence. There was no screaming or clambering on to the stage; the group were treated with unmistakable respect and appreciation was shown in the traditional way — enthusiastic clapping.

Unlike the modern trend, the Cream do not rely on complicated melodies and impressive harmonies to get an effective sound. They have no time for gimmicks—their sole concern is to produce good music.

Their strength lies in their instrumentals, but bass player Jack Bruce produced a groovy bluesy style of singing to liven up the numbers.

"It is a 'never been heard before' type music," explained the skilful blues guitarist, Eric Clapton. "It's new, but not brand new." Jazz, blues and classical all contributed to the new sound.

"It's changed from its original concept and it's still developing," Eric went on. "We just want to play the best

there is, to play and be better than anyone else."

And, judging from their reception in Hull, they're more than halfway to reaching their ambition.

Eric, however, was disappointed with the response. "By normal standards we get standing ovations and encores for hours. But here we just went on and off—they obviously weren't overwhelmed.

"Perhaps if we had a record in the charts and they knew us better we might have got more applause," he added.

But he was wrong. Everyone was impressed, and superlatives referring to the group were tossed about the dance hall during, and long after, the time the boys were on stage.

Local tie

And perhaps Hull can feel justifiably proud of The Cream, for the city can claim a family connection with the drummer, long-haired Ginger Baker.

His wife, Elizabeth, is the grand-daughter of the 90-year-old Mexican Consul, Mr William Hopper, and his wife, Alice.

Ginger, Elizabeth and their six-year-old daughter, Ginette, stayed with Mr and Mrs Hopper, and they also seized the opportunity of visiting other relations in the city during their stay in Hull.

What does Mr Hopper think of the career of his grand-daughter's husband? "He doesn't mention it," Ginger admitted with a grin, "I don't think he likes it.

But British teenagers certainly do.

An afternoon in the park.

Eric dubbed the new sound, 'blues, ancient and modern,' but surprisingly, he wasn't sure whether audiences would accept Cream. "I don't believe we'll ever get over to them. People will always listen with biased ears and preconceived ideas, remembering us individually as we used to be."

His theory, however, was undeniably squashed when the three took over The Graham Bond circuit and drew crowds that literally spilled onto the street. From receiving £45.00 a gig, within a few months they were commanding more than £100.00 every night on the university circuit.

That September Cream went into Mayfair Sound to record (in just ten days) their first album, the bluesy *Fresh Cream*, comprising mainly re-

what I wanted to hear."

Meanwhile, as *Fresh Cream* raced up the UK charts to number 6, by early 1967 the band decided it was high time to conquer America. A March appearance on 'Murray the K's Easter Rock'n'Roll Extravaganza' at New York's RKO Theater put them on the map. Sharing the bill with Wilson Pickett, Simon and Garfunkel and The Who, the show was all in all a prestigious affair.

"We took the gig as a joke," Eric revealed. "There was no chance for Ginger to play his solo and we had to use The Who's equipment because we couldn't take any with us."

According to Clapton, the band indulged in some wild, off stage chicanery with their rivals from West London. Eric recalls, "We had fourteen-pound bags of flour and eggs we were going to use on stage. Unfortunately, Murray somehow heard about it and said we wouldn't get paid if we did. So instead we spread everything around the dressing rooms. Pete Townshend ended up swimming fully clothed in a foot of water when his shower overflowed."

On the heels of that appearance Cream went into New York's Atlantic Studios to record their second album, *Disraeli Gears*. The proceedings got off to a decidedly sour start when Atlantic chairman, Ahmet Ertegan, told Jack Bruce, "Eric should be the lead singer and composer. You are

Left to right: Eric Clapton, Jack Bruce and Ginger Baker in 1967.

only the bass player."

As Baker tells it, the directive only made the ambitious Bruce more determined to maintain his position as frontman: "Every day he would arrive with at least five songs. Anything Eric and I put forward was instantly thwarted by Jack insisting, 'But that's not finished, man. I've got this one all done.'"

Eric commented, "My way of introducing material was just to play it. After the fights died down at rehearsal I'd be playing a riff and one of them would go, 'Well, maybe we could do that.'"

"It was very tense and hesitant stuff, a situation where I hadn't the confidence or experience to stand up and dictate what we were going to do. When it came down to forceful personalities Ginger and Jack were vying for the role. So I just let them get on with it and backed off."

Clapton did manage a credit though, for his ambitious *Tales of Brave Ulysses*, marked by his initial use of the wah-wah pedal, a lead followed by Jimi Hendrix on his compelling *Burning of the Midnight Lamp*.

The album's anchor, *Sunshine of Your Love*, prompted Eric to dub Cream, "One of the first heavy metal bands without knowing it." Though

Baker claims that both he and Clapton contributed to the composition - Eric providing the middle eight chords - once again the credit went entirely to Bruce/Brown. This was an early example of the problems which caused the band's ultimate demise.

Soon afterwards, the trio arrived back in London to learn of an exciting new development. Beatles manager, Brian Epstein, had joined forces with Robert Stigwood to form NEMS Stigwood Productions and one of Epstein's first moves was to book Cream into his trendy Saville Theatre on Shaftesbury Avenue in London for a dramatic production. Six banks of triple stacked Marshall speakers were lined up at the rear of the stage.

In the show's deafening finale, one of Clapton's guitars was dramatical-

Certainly not as photogenic as many other bands, Cream more than made up for it in raw musicianship.

ly suspended on swinging chains from the ceiling. As it slowly descended Eric would grab it, strike a final chord and feed it back through the speakers. More guitars would float down and the pattern was repeated while the crowd roared.

Despite the enthusiastic response to the band's live performances, Clapton was later to comment, "When Cream became acknowledged as virtuosos, that's when the rot set in, because we started to believe it

Above: Back to the park for yet another publicity shot ....

Opposite: Inspired by Hendrix's frizzy head of hair, Clapton soon had his own naturally straight hair permed.

and became very cynical."

On 27th August, in the wake of Epstein's tragic death, the band departed for a demanding four month American tour. "One that would make and break the band," Bruce was to confess later.

Landing center stage in the dreamy, psychedelic 'summer of love,' Cream's timing couldn't have been better. Their debut at San Francisco's

legendary Fillmore West ushered in Cream's hallmark improvisational jam style, never before attempted in a rock setting.

"Prior to Fillmore," explains Jack, "we did three and five minute versions of songs. But when we got to San Francisco there was such a loose feeling about the whole thing. The audience was shouting 'Just play!' so we started to improvise, to lengthen solos and go along with the feeling."

Cream x 3 in October, 1967.

Carlos Santana was on hand for the event. "The *Fresh Cream* album sounded so fantastic for being just three people. But they sounded even better than the album the night I saw them. They looked like giants, like they were on stilts or something."

"They were the first blues based power trio," added Bill Graham, the Fillmore's owner, "but with that powerful rock and roll guitar they absolutely destroyed the place."

The original bad boys of psychedelic rock.

Cream were suddenly the hottest ticket of the year, playing their progressive rock at sold-out venues coast to coast. "I never played better in my life," Clapton was saying. "More is expected of me in Cream. I have to play rhythm guitar as well as lead. I'm no longer trying to play anything other than like a white man."

MORE CREAM

STRANGE BREW
SUNSHINE OF YOUR LOVE
TALES OF BRAVE ULYSSES
S.W.L.A.B.R.
DANCE THE NIGHT AWAY
TAKE IT BACK
BLUE CONDITION
WE'RE GOING WRONG

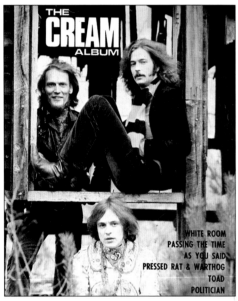

WHITE ROOM
PASSING THE TIME
AS YOU SAID
PRESSED RAT & WARTHOG
TOAD
POLITICIAN

Cream at the dizzy height of their phenomenal success.

However, according to Ben Palmer, a roadie with the band at that time, it was Jack Bruce who really stretched Clapton as a musician. "On those long Cream numbers, when each played a solo, Eric was pushed by Jack as far as anybody ever pushed him."

"To the point," adds Clapton, "where it was really just a battle, a war. He has to clear a space around him and you can't get very close a lot of the time."

By the end of 1967 Cream was a superstar act trapped in a web of stifling commercialism, greed and the well-oiled Stigwood machine. They'd no sooner come off the road than they were back in the studio in February to produce their third and most successful album, *Wheels of Fire*, driven by the thundering, mystical *White Room*. Released in mid 1968, *Wheels of Fire* was a double album including the best of the live Fillmore West sets.

Mentally and physically exhausted, Cream went back on the road working the American stadium circuit, the band on the edge of burnout. Playing before enormous crowds in cavernous arenas, their performances had gone from creative set to commercial spectacle.

Recalls Baker, "Our success gained a life of its own. We were so big audiences didn't care what we played or even if we played. As long as we showed up and produced a riot of noise, they were satisfied. For top shelf creative musicians like the three of us, this was the sounding of the death knell. Cream had become a caricature of itself."

The overwhelming crowd noise coupled with poor sound systems eventually took a toll. Baker had to cover his hands in plasters, blistered from pounding his drum kit, while Clapton suffered a profound hearing loss.

"I was wearing specially designed earplugs because I couldn't hear any more. I was playing full volume in a kind of weird traumatic state knowing that I had to play and not really wanting to. I was really brought down."

Meanwhile, clashes between Baker and Bruce flared yet again, escalating to the point where the members of the band booked into separate hotels and barely even spoke to one another.

Clapton observed, "They were chemically polarized and I had to be the mediator. Their anger was so vicious, the venom so powerful it could reduce anyone to tears. Between Jack and Ginger it was pure love-hate. This was a big band going out of anybody's control."

The endless adulation, notes Clapton, was also beginning to wear thin. "We really didn't have a band with Cream. We rarely played as an ensemble. We were three virtuosos, soloing all the time. I was flying high on an ego trip. I was pretty sure I was the best thing happening that was popular."

A key moment came when the 11th May, 1968 issue of *Rolling Stone* ran a cover article bearing the headline, "Will Cream's Music Stand the Test of Time?" The effect on Clapton was profound.

"The review said how boring and repetitive our performance had become, how I was the master of the cliché. And it was true! We'd been flying with blinkers for so long we weren't aware of the changes that were taking place musically. New people were coming up and growing and we were simply repeating ourselves, living on legend, a year or two out of date. The ring of truth just knocked me backwards. I was in a restaurant and I fainted. After I woke up, I immediately decided it was the end of the band."

According to Jack Bruce, however, there were far more selfish reasons why Clapton wanted out: "Eric always wanted to be a star. When he played on The Beatles' *White Album* and when he got involved working with George Harrison, he thought he should leave us behind."

The band fulfilled their final commitments, a farewell six week US tour in October and one final album. At this point Bruce, Baker and Clapton were reduced to laying down their parts individually on the appropriately titled *Goodbye Cream* album. Clapton's contribution was the breezy *Badge* co-written with George Harrison.

"It was sort of about a girlfriend. George wrote "bridge" on this piece of paper and I was reading it upside down and said, 'Oh, you've called it Badge, that's a good name.' It means nothing."

The brief, airy tune backed by Harrison's rolling rhythm guitar featured a compact solo that would become a hallmark of Clapton's subsequent work.

Cream's farewell appearance at London's Royal Albert Hall on 26th November (supported by Yes and Taste) coincided with *Wheels of Fire* achieving platinum status. Clapton discloses that he did have second thoughts about disbanding Cream, especially after being heavily influenced by The Band's lighter, more funky *Music From the Big Pink* album.

"If only we had a keyboard player, or could play a bit differently. I felt I wanted to change Cream, but it wasn't up to me. I wasn't the leader of the band and I didn't know how to change it even if I could persuade Jack and Ginger. I was frustrated. That's why I faced up to a split."

Even as he was licking his wounds, Clapton was about to jump into another supergroup - a move which was to set in motion a series of problems with far-reaching and damaging consequences, from which Clapton didn't really recover until about fifteen years later.

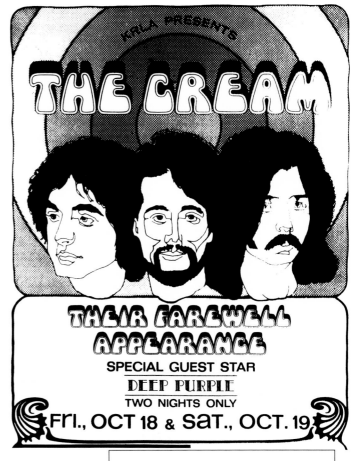

Cream's last hurrah.

CHAPTER FOUR

EDGE OF DARKNESS: BLIND FAITH AND DEREK AND THE DOMINOS

"Part of my character is made up of an obsession to push something to the limit. Life's like a razor blade. I'll always walk along the edge."
Eric Clapton

Clapton once termed the all-star Blind Faith, "The only real regret I have. It was so short-lived we didn't ever really groove. That whole thing was very transparent. I mean, it's almost not there."

The idea took root in the blossoming friendship between Eric and singer, guitarist and keyboard player, Steve Winwood, over the winter of 1968-69. Winwood, a precocious talent still only twenty years old, had just disbanded the progressive band Traffic, and he found a sympathetic comrade in Clapton, who was similarly in mourning over Cream's demise.

Explains Winwood, "One day Eric came down to the house in Berkshire where I was living and we had a play. I said it would be nice to get back to the old feeling, when he jammed with my first band, The Spencer Davis Group."

Clapton immediately saw the opportunity to follow through on his idea to add a keyboards player to Cream. After jamming at Winwood's remote cottage for several weeks, the two agreed to enlist the aid of a drummer and officially form a trio. They were casting about for likely candidates, when who should show up at Winwood's door one rainy afternoon but Ginger Baker.

Baker recalls that first impromptu session with great enthusiasm. "We hadn't played five minutes before we dared look at one another with giant grins signifying instant musical rapport. Steve's superb mastery of the keyboard was eclipsed only by an impeccable sense of timing, one hundred per cent perfection. It was the timing that gave Stevie such an innate feel for jazz."

Winwood, similarly impressed with the drummer's dynamic, intricate,

Opposite: Blind Faith.
Left to right: Ginger Baker, Rick Grech, Eric Clapton and Steve Winwood at Clapton's country home.

BLIND FAITH

ALBUM No1   7'6

Opposite: More bombastic blues
from Old Clapper.

yet delicate style very much wanted Baker in the band. A disillusioned Clapton, however, concluded that the group was doomed from the start. "Steve couldn't see it this way, but when Ginger walked, in I lost interest. Steve and I would play and hang out for days on end just enjoying one another's company. The next thing I know Ginger was knocking on the door. Now I love Ginger very much, but at that time I didn't really want him around. I was still grieving for Cream and wanted no part of Cream again. But I didn't have the heart to say no."

Baker added, "I didn't realize until years later that Eric didn't want me in the band."

Once word leaked out, the publicity hype revved up in anticipation of this new 'super-group' which inspired Clapton sarcastically to dub the band Blind Faith. The group was immediately signed to Island Records and began recording at Olympic Studios. A bass player was needed to complete their sound, and Rick Grech of Family was recruited. A competent, if not outstanding bassist, Grech was signed because of his ability on the electric violin. Grech was the first to use this instrument in a pop music context.

The line-up finalised, it became urgent to put out an album as soon as possible. With the able Rolling Stones' producer, Jimmy Miller, on board, some six tracks were recorded over just ten days. Winwood dubbed the album "a conglomeration of everything: blues, jazz, rock,

Below: Eric in the seventies.

pop, folk, even Indian music."

This project sound was a wonderful showcase for Eric, who did some beautiful harpsichord-like picking on the melancholy *Can't Find My Way Home*. His lone composition, *Presence of the Lord*, is a classy exploration of atonality accomplished in a blues idiom on his new Gibson Firebird. Another highlight of the album is an excellent reworking of Buddy Holly's *Well All Right*.

"I think the music may have sailed right over people's heads," Eric later surmised, "but I still like it. It was one of the nicest things I ever did."

The album, simply called *Blind Faith*, was released in August, selling a staggering 450,000 copies in its first week, hitting the top of the album charts on both sides of the Atlantic and becoming a million seller in just one month. However, the original UK album cover, which depicted a young, nude girl holding a silver airplane, was considered too controversial for release in the USA. Rumored to be Baker's daughter, Netti, the girl was in fact, the child of a friend of cover photographer, Bob Ciderman.

If nothing else, Blind Faith was an exercise in expediency. With little time for preparation, the band made their public debut on 7th June, 1969 in London's Hyde Park, before 150,000 eager and well-behaved fans. However, the performance met with only a lukewarm response from the critics. *Melody Maker* called the band "under-rehearsed" and "very much like Steve Winwood with a back-up group."

Following a brief eight date tour of Scandinavia on the modest club circuit, Blind Faith, encouraged by greedy promoters, was thrown into an American tour opening on 12th July, 1969 at Madison Square Garden. The show, with its deplorable sound system, sparked off an ugly, destructive riot which cut short the performance.

Said Clapton, "The crowd came prepared for the fact that there would be cops and were prepared to be bugged from the start. The main thing was to heckle the cops. The cops replied with violence."

The episode set the tone for the remainder of the tour and the band also suffered additional problems. Lack of material forced the group to perform hits from their combined repertoire. Winwood admitted, "We failed because we couldn't resist requests for the hits. Ginger chucked in an old Cream song, I put in a Traffic song and the identity of the band was killed stone dead."

Performing with Blind Faith had an especially depressing effect on Clapton. On stage he appeared lethargic and disinterested. According to Baker, "He was folding up on us." The picture of a despondent musician groping for his bearings is supported by two significant developments that occurred midway through the tour.

One night, Clapton encountered a pair of zealous Born Again Christians in his dressing room and proclaimed himself "saved". He also struck up a serious friendship with Blind Faith's back-up band, the blues act Delaney and

Opposite: Laying down the law on stage in the early seventies.

Overleaf: Two views from the Rolling Stones' Rock'n'Roll Circus in December, 1968.

Above: Blind Faith live in sunny Baltimore.

John Lennon jams in aid of UNICEF at the London Lyceum Ballroom on 15th December, 1969.
Left to right: Eric Clapton, drummer Alan White and John Lennon.

Bonnie, electing to travel with them and even joining them on stage. At one point he told Baker, "They should be top of the bill. They're much better than we are."

Clapton later admitted: "I was looking for a way out from the minute we hit the road. Every group I've been in got to a critical point where it either had to get better or break up. I started looking for somewhere else to go and Delaney and Bonnie were a godsend. They were instrumental in the breaking up of Blind Faith, or of me leaving, because I was so enthused about the style of their material and where they came from."

After their final performance on 24th August, 1969, in Honolulu, the band drifted on their separate ways. In a sad post-mortem on the band, Winwood admitted: "We did not sound good live due to the simple lack of experience being a group. We had no natural growth and it was very evident on stage."

Adds Clapton: "It was all very frail. When we were rehearsing, it was just me and Steve, a fun-type jazz thing. When we started recording

Another view of what Lennon cleverly dubbed The Plastic Ono Super Group.

A snappy group shot following the gig.

though, it changed. Then Ginger took the reins and could see the bucks. So could Robert Stigwood. Before we knew it we were into the harrassment of making a record and a tour with no desire to do so. When we went on stage it was already over somehow. It was already dead."

In an abrupt change of pace Eric joined John Lennon in Toronto in mid-September 1969 for a rock'n'roll revival. He also recorded with The Plastic Ono Band on their *Cold Turkey* single and participated as part of the Plastic Ono Supergroup in the December 'Peace for Christmas'

UNICEF concert at London's Lyceum Ballroom with an all-star line-up, including Billy Preston, Keith Moon, George Harrison and Bonzo Dog Band drummer, 'Legs' Larry Smith.

Delaney and Bonnie Bramlett, meanwhile, remained Clapton's most influential creative force until the end of 1969 and into 1970. A US tour, 'Delaney and Bonnie and Friends,' partly financed by Clapton, included appearances by Dave Mason, George Harrison, Rita Coolidge and Bobby Keyes, as well as Clapton himself, in the more comfortable, less pressurized role of celebrated sideman.

The Bramletts' creative input loomed large on Clapton's first solo album recorded in Los Angeles and simply entitled *Eric Clapton*. The songs featured much understated guitar work on Clapton's less strident Fender

On tour with Delaney and Bonnie in 1969. George Harrison made a guest appearance on the tour.

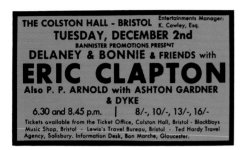

From the time he met them, Clapton was a fan of the R&B inspired Delaney & Bonnie, and, as a result, undertook a great deal of live work with the group.

Stratocaster. Critics though, were not kind; *Melody Maker* charged that Clapton had "submerged himself to the point where it really does become a Delaney and Bonnie album."

The album did produce the driving, gospel-tinged hit single, *After Midnight*, a rocking J.J. Cale number which unveiled Eric's improved, more confident vocal technique and the tight, spirited guitar riffs which would mark his later work.

Clapton then followed up the record with a bold experiment. Together with members of the Bramletts' band, Eric went undercover as Derek and The Dominos for a 1970-1971 UK and US club tour. "It was funny, because no one knew who we were. But word spread very quickly and we had a good crowd most of the time."

The core of Derek and the Dominos was Eric Clapton (guitar and vocals), Carl Radle (bass), Bobby Whitlock (keyboards and some vocals) and Jim Gordon (drums). Dave Mason played guitar in a single charity concert for Dr. Benjamin Spock's Civil Liberties Fund and Duane Allman joined in on guitar in the recording of the *Layla* album.

Eric's legacy from the brief Derek and the Dominos period is his tortured, soul-stripping lament of unrequited love, the unforgettable *Layla*. Written in April, 1970, in the midst of the most famous love triangle in rock history - Eric, torn between his loyalty to best friend, George Harrison, and his love for Harrison's beautiful fashion model wife, Pattie Boyd - it must be one of the greatest rock love songs of all time.

Admitting that he wrote the passionate song in a desperate attempt to capture Pattie's attention, Clapton claimed that when he played it for her, "she didn't give a damn."

Pattie, however, tells a quite different story: "He played *Layla* to me two or three times. His intensity was both frightening and fascinating. It was a very powerful record. I was puzzled, flattered, shocked and amazed. I had no idea it would occur to him to write a song for me."

The single emerged from the album *Layla and Other Assorted Love Songs*, and, despite the fact that he refused to have his name anywhere on the sleeve, it is among the highlights of Clapton's career. The catalyst for the project, according to Eric, were the stirring slide guitar licks of Duane Allman. "I'd heard Duane on Wilson Pickett's *Hey Jude* and he blew me away. After the concert I invited him back to the studio and he stayed. We fell in love and an album took off from there."

Allman noted: "I was just going to play on one or two sides and then, as we kept on going, it kept developing. I'm as proud of that as any album I've ever been on. I'm as satisfied with my work on that as I could possibly be."

However, towards the end of 1970, a series of tragic episodes began which would propel Clapton into one of the bleakest periods of his life. On the night of 17th September Eric planned to meet Jimi Hendrix at the Lyceum Ballroom to see Sly Stone in concert. With him he had a rare, left-handed Stratocaster guitar which he intended to present to Jimi, who often had to resort to restringing a regular guitar and playing it upside-down. But Hendrix never showed up. It was not until the next day that Clapton learned of Jimi's tragic death from an overdose of barbiturates and he was heartbroken.

"I just had this terrible, lonely feeling. I loved Jimi and his music and I'd played with him. I went out in the garden and cried all day. Not because he'd gone, but because he hadn't taken me with him. It just made me so angry. I wasn't sad, I was just pissed off."

Just six weeks later came the equally sad news that his beloved grandfather, Jack Clapp, had died of cancer. Then, a few months later, Duane Allman lost his life in a motorcycle accident. All in all, not really a very happy time for the sensitive, introspective musician

During The Dominos' American tour at the end of 1970, Clapton was barely holding on. Playing in cavernous arenas with fans screaming out his name forced him to re-live the familiar rock star nightmare. Yet, even as the band filled venues to capacity, paradoxically the *Layla* album, released in November, failed to chart in the UK and only made number 16 in the US charts. It wasn't until two years later that the single was re-released and achieved classic status.

Before ending up as Mrs Clapton, Pattie Boyd was a top London fashion model. She is seen here strutting her stuff with Twiggy.

Pattie Boyd and her first husband, George Harrison, on their wedding day.

For the grieving Clapton, it was all too much to handle. Shunning friends and family, he retreated into seclusion in his Surrey home and began a harrowing three year period of heroin addiction. Although Jack Bruce termed his problem "a very tiny habit," those closest to the guitarist testify otherwise.

One of Clapton's oldest and best friends, Ben Palmer, recalls, "It was the worst experience I'd encountered. I saw a man who was very dear to me and he was clearly killing himself."

For Rose the realization was one of shocked disbelief: "He'd stand in the doorway looking tired out. It didn't even seem like Rick. Then my daughter said, 'Mum, he's on drugs.' I used to really pray, get down on my hands and knees for Eric. I tried to talk to him, but he just laughed."

Harrison and Bob Dylan. The album's country/pop direction had a lively toe-tapping feel, but Clapton's playing was uneven and outshone by Robbie Robertson's solo on *Sign Language*.

Although Eric later claimed the out-takes were superior to the album's official tracks, critics pronounced Clapton as "suffering from a severe identity crisis and running out of steam."

In 1976 the South American percussionist, Sergio Pashora, briefly joined Eric's live band. Clapton appeared in The Band's farewell concert, The Last Waltz, and he contributed to albums by Joe Cocker, Stephen Bishop and Ringo Starr.

1977, however, proved a landmark year for Clapton, as he bounced back into the limelight with his monster album, *Slowhand*. This time

65

Opposite and below: Eric and Pattie, a love made in heaven, and, later, unmade in the courts.

HELLO

Me and the Mrs. got married the other day, but that
was in America, so we've decided to have a bash in
my garden on Saturday May 19th about 3.00 p.m.
for all our mates here at home, if you are free, try
and make it, it's bound to be a laugh
......see you then.....
Eric and Pattie Clapton

P.S.
You don't have to
bring any presents
if you don't
want to.

Above: Pattie and Eric Clapton invite friends to their wedding reception back home in England, after getting married in Tucson, Arizona.

around he captured a whole new audience, won over by the record's unrestrained romanticism underscored by subtle country picking inspired by Don Williams and rejuvenated sparkling riffs on Clapton's favorite Strat (an amalgamation of several vintage models nicknamed 'Blackie'). The album, released in November, became Clapton's biggest hit to date, reaching number 2 in the US album charts and spawning three top 10 hits: the gentle, floating *Lay Down Sally*, J.J. Cale's gritty and often misunderstood *Cocaine* and Eric's classic ballad for Pattie, *Wonderful Tonight*.

He explains the genesis of the song: "Pattie was getting ready to go out. We were about two hours late. I went upstairs to see what was going on and she was up there with one of her girlfriends still trying on different things. I said, 'Well that's nice - what is it, a curtain? You look wonderful.' "

"I went back downstairs and while I was waiting I picked up the guitar and started writing that song. It was written just to pass the time and I was pretty angry."

The song took on a different light when, on 28th March, 1979, Eric dragged a beaming Pattie on stage in Tucson, Arizona to croon the ballad to his new bride before an ecstatic crowd. The couple had just been married the day before at Tucson's Apostolic Assembly of Faith in Christ Jesus.

It was a toss-up whether Clapton was more elated by marrying Pattie or the kick-off of a forty date US tour with blues idol, Muddy Waters, on board. Eric had hero worshipped Muddy since his teens, and, as a result, was initially tongue-tied in the presence of the blues legend. He even refused to touch Waters' guitar.

"It's absolutely taboo for me," he explained. "When I heard Muddy for the first time I knew that was it. He was the first blues man to really get down into me, really into my soul. He has always made me feel this was the end of the road, as good as it could get."

As the tour progressed, the two struck up a deeply personal relationship. "Short of actually going to the court house, he was my father," says Eric. "He'd scold me, give me advice like any father would. He kept hammering it home to me that there was nothing wrong with being a blues musician, that blues playing is beautiful because it's from the inside out."

At the end of the tour Clapton returned home for a grand wedding reception on 19th May in the grounds of his Surrey home. In attendance were The Rolling Stones and the other members of Cream, as well as Lonnie Donegan, Denny Laine, David Bowie and Elton John. The highlight of the event was an all-star jam session in the marquee which included the first reunion of the three Beatles (minus John Lennon). The caliber of the music, however, was debatable.

Ginger Baker recalls, "I played drums along with Ringo and at one remarkable point, when three of The Beatles took the stage together, it was me backing them. The music was really happening."

Baker's daughter Netti disagreed. "They were playing the hits and then Mick Jagger sang Miss You, sounding absolutely diabolical. All these aspiring musicians who think these superstars sound so great when they get together to jam...well, they don't!"

Pattie and Eric disappeared early in the evening to begin their married life. A hit album, a successful tour and now marriage to the woman whom he had loved from afar for so long. Clapton was riding a high that simply couldn't last.

CHAPTER SIX

WORLD OF PAIN: PERSONAL LIFE

"My dedication to music has driven everyone away. I've had girlfriends, but I've ended up on my own. I used to find that lonesome image very attractive, very bluesy, but now I'm stuck with it whether I like it or not."
Eric Clapton

Despite renewed success with the ultra-commercial *Slowhand*, by 1980 Clapton recognized that he was wandering into a musical no-man's land. He admitted, "*Slowhand* was a very "nervous" album, maybe because of the lack of material we had. It was lightweight, really lightweight; we were so sort of limp about it that it was lazy."

Even"so, he continued sliding back into the 'less is more' approach, rooted in Delaney and Bonnie's delicate rhythms from a decade earlier. His relaxed, often laconic guitar meanderings through the Tulsa influenced *Backless* album featured a country/western touch far removed from Clapton's earlier blues sound. Only the driving duet with co-writer Marcy Levy on *Roll It* conveyed any real intensity.

In a desperate quest for change Eric turned over his entire American band and replaced them with an all-British corp of top session players, including close friend, Gary Brooker (ex Procol Harum) on keyboards and respected guitarist, Albert Lee. A move that would prove unwise. Although the ensemble's first outing on the live *Just One Night* album (recorded in Tokyo) was lifted by Clapton's energized solos and hit number 3 in the UK and number 2 in the US, the follow-up studio album, *Another Ticket*, exposed the limits of mainstream musicians ill-equipped to tackle the blues. Apart from the exceptional blues rendition of Sleepy John Estes' *Floating Bridge* and the riveting single, *I Can't Stand It*, the project was largely uninspired and without direction.

If Clapton wasn't exactly singing the blues, he was certainly living them. By the early eighties his profound drinking had escalated to an extreme as devastating and life-threatening as his former heroin addiction. The severity of the problem revealed itself in the 1979 documentary 'Eric Clapton's Rolling Hotel,' showing the guitarist with slurred speech and in poor physical condition.

Gary Brooker recalls, "There were tears in his eyes on some occasions. He'd say to me 'I'm cracking up.'"

"The only certainty was that Eric would be in a permanent alcoholic

Opposite: Playing to an audience has always been very important for Clapton and the development of his music. Here he is at yet another in a long list of never-ending gigs in the mid eighties.

Out on the prowl after a searing show somewhere on the road.

Above: Playing piggy-in-the-middle between two well turned out bodyguards.

Left: With close mate, Clive Griffin.

Opposite: Living the blues on stage.

trayal of what I could do in all the areas I play in. There was a little reggae, a little acoustic blues and a lot more of my playing that Roland guitar synthesizer sounding like a saxophone. We were very satisfied with it as a concept album, showing the different sides of me."

Behind the Sun featured the fiery *Same Old Blues*, which captured some of Clapton's finest licks ever. Critics and fans alike considered it amongst the artist's greatest moments on record.

"It has one of those prolonged guitar breaks and chord changes, for a blues, which lift it out a rut," explains Clapton.

The record company, Warner, however, felt that the album didn't contain enough "singles material" and flew Clapton out to Los Angeles to record additional material with top-line session players like Toto drummer, Jeff Porcaro and Fleetwood Mac's Lindsey Buckingham. The sessions produced the blustery hit, *Forever Man*.

Behind The Sun was released in March of 1985, which was also the year Clapton turned forty - a milestone which he embraced passionately. "Turning forty was the nicest thing to happen to me in years because I'd had a desperate need to become something other than what I was. I am very much a chameleon. I can be altered and changed beyond recognition. But I can accept it more now, I'm a lot happier with what I am."

Fit and invigorated, Clapton seemed to be everywhere, granting interviews to all the top music magazines, appearing on talk shows and

En route to the prestigious BPI Awards in London during the late eighties.

Below and opposite: Clapton with his long-time girlfriend, Lori Del Santo, mother of his son, Conor.

embarking on tours of Europe and America. He had re-dedicated himself to the blistering caliber of playing fans hadn't witnessed in years, even introducing to his sets the Cream classic, *White Room*, which he hadn't performed in seventeen years.

1985 was also the year of the transcontinental 'Live Aid' concert, to raise money for African famine relief. Appearing at Philadelphia's JFK Stadium on 13th July in front of 90,000 fans, not to mention the worldwide television audience of 1.5 billion, Clapton launched into *White Room* with a shattering wah wah solo and topped off the set with the now classic *Layla* with Phil Collins backing him on drums. In the finale, Eric joined the largest assembly of star musicians ever assembled for the emotional *We Are The World*.

Maintaining his energy and continued good fortune right into 1986, Clapton once more changed gears. This time recruiting yet again, Nathan East (bass) and Greg Philliganes (keyboards), young guns from the *Behind the Sun* sessions, along with Phil Collins, to work on his new album. They booked time in LA's Sunset Sound Studios to produce the album which, at that point, was titled *One More Car, One More Rider*.

Teamed up with talented, though dominating, songwriter, Jerry 'wild man' Williams, Clapton demonstrated his growing 'take charge' confidence. "Two years ago," he confided, "I would have been completely submerged by him. My personality up until recently would have quite happily stepped aside and let him take the lead role. This time it didn't happen. I was very firm in making sure this record was for me."

Here was a powerful sweep of material with a band that could interpret both blues and jazz. Tina Turner's guest spot on two numbers, *Tearing Us Apart* and *Hold On*, gave Clapton's studio performance a kick he hadn't shown in years.

In a sharp twist of irony the album's title was changed to *August* in celebration of the birth of Clapton's son, Conor, by Italian television personality, Lori Del Santo. The event was sadly a public pronouncement that his fifteen year relationship with Pattie had now come to an end. Having endured the intense pressures of alcoholism and fame, their fragile marriage was unable to withstand this final blow.

According to Ginger Baker: "His affair with Lori proved ultimately too much for Pattie. Suddenly Eric had the son he always wanted, which left Pattie - apparently unable to have children - devastated."

Clapton also has a 9-year-old daughter, who was born while he was still married to Pattie. His daughter, Ruth, was a well kept secret for many years before Clapton acknowledged her existence in public.

Of the breakup Eric said, "Our separation was a sort of mutual agreement. As far as what happened with us, the problems were on both sides. I probably definitely instigated it in many areas. It was best that

we got divorced. With the birth of Conor it was impossible for Pattie. I probably would have struggled to keep the whole thing going, juggling like crazy, but it would have driven someone mad, probably me."

The pain of the split was exposed in Eric's declaration, "Pattie is the only woman I have ever really loved."

CHAPTER SEVEN

TEARS IN HEAVEN: SAYING GOODBYE

"I wonder, 'Why me? Why have I survived?' I have to look at that as the positive. I have survived these things and therefore I've got some kind of responsibility to remain creative and not dwell on the misfortune of it all."

Eric Clapton

As his divorce was finalized in 1988, Clapton was celebrating his twenty-fifth anniversary in the music business. To mark the occasion Polygram issued *Crossroads*, an impressive boxed set tracing his remarkable career. It contains not only a quarter century of hits and great album tracks, but a bounty of unreleased material.

"I think I'm beginning to relax more at what I do," the guitarist said, marking the milestone. "I don't feel I have to prove anything and I still really do enjoy the work."

A highly visible, ever stylish Clapton was branching out, playing at just about every charity show, culminating in the 'Nelson Mandela 70th Birthday Party Concert.' This concert was played to an audience of 80,000 fans in June at Wembley and included performances by an array of stars including George Michael, Dire Straits and Sting.

In addition, Clapton turned film composer, which began with a couple of tunes for the 1987 film, *Color of Money* with Tom Cruise and Paul Newman, including the stirring top 40 hit, *It's In The Way That You Use It*. He continued this success by doing music for Phil Collins' *Buster*, Mickey Rourke's *Homeboy* and the smash action thriller, *Lethal Weapon*.

The nineties proved to be both the best and worst of times for Clapton. He began the decade with a series of ambitious concerts at the Royal Albert Hall in London. This series of concerts was divided into several different musical formats, including a quartet, a big band and his personal favorite, blues nights, with guitarist Robert Cray, whom Clapton once lauded as "the finest touch player in the world."

He relied heavily, much to the delight of sold-out audiences, on material from his latest work, the critically acclaimed, multi-platinum *Journeyman*. After a decade of wandering, this was Clapton coming home to his roots, playing to his strengths, shaking off the demons with Bo Diddley's fiery blues stomp, *Before You Accuse Me* and the riveting chart hit, *Pretending*.

Opposite: A view of Clapton in the early nineties.

On stage with guitar favourite, Albert Lee.

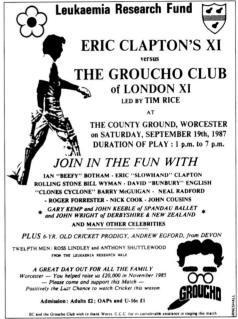

Leukaemia Research Fund

ERIC CLAPTON'S XI
versus
THE GROUCHO CLUB
of LONDON XI
LED BY TIM RICE
AT
THE COUNTY GROUND, WORCESTER
on SATURDAY, SEPTEMBER 19th, 1987
DURATION OF PLAY : 1 p.m. to 7 p.m.

JOIN IN THE FUN WITH

IAN "BEEFY" BOTHAM - ERIC "SLOWHAND" CLAPTON
ROLLING STONE BILL WYMAN · DAVID "BUNBURY" ENGLISH
"CLONES CYCLONE" BARRY McGUIGAN - NEAL RADFORD
- ROGER FORRESTER - NICK COOK · JOHN COUSINS
*GARY KEMP and JOHN KEEBLE of SPANDAU BALLET
and JOHN WRIGHT of DERBYSHIRE & NEW ZEALAND*
AND MANY OTHER CELEBRITIES

PLUS 6-YR. OLD CRICKET PRODIGY, ANDREW EGFORD, from DEVON

TWELFTH MEN: ROSS LINDLEY and ANTHONY SHUTTLEWOOD
FROM THE LEUKAEMIA RESEARCH WALK

A GREAT DAY OUT FOR ALL THE FAMILY
Worcester — You helped raise us £20,000 in November 1985
— Please come and support this Match —
Positively the Last Chance to watch Cricket this season

Admission: Adults £2; OAPs and U-16s £1

EC and the Groucho Club wish to thank Worcs. C.C.C. for its considerable assistance in staging this match

GROUCHO

Above: Out for a pleasant day of cricket, a lifelong passion for Clapton.

"I had a subconscious feeling that we didn't want this album to be filled with too many similar tracks," says Eric. "I will deliberately choose a lot of opposites if I'm given complete control, which my producer, Russ Tittelman gave me." Clapton also credited the ace producer with his stronger vocal delivery which rings through on the album.

Then tragedy struck. Winding up a US tour in East Troy, Wisconsin,

ONLY UK APPEARANCE

ERIC CLAPTON
and His Band
featuring

PHIL COLLINS - drums
NATHAN EAST - bass
GREG PHILLINGANES
keyboards

PLUS SPECIAL GUESTS
THE ROBERT CRAY BAND

BIRMINGHAM NEC
MONDAY 14th JULY 1986

TICKETS £11.00 £12.50 ON SALE SAT 7th JUNE 4 TICKETS ONLY PER PERSON
FROM BIRMINGHAM NEC BOX OFFICE & CREDIT CARD HOTLINE 021 780 4133
LONDON KEITH PROWSE SHOPS & CREDIT CARD HOTLINE 01 748 1414
(Subject to Booking fee)

Right and opposite: Making the scene at yet
another music awards extravaganza.

Clapton had just completed a performance with blues rocker, Stevie Ray Vaughan, on the 26th August. Vaughan, along with Eric's bodyguard, his US booking agent and assistant tour manager, Colin Smythe, were killed when their helicopter crashed into a ski slope in heavy fog. A shocked and saddened Clapton called it: "A tragic loss of my companions, associates and friends. The worst thing for me was that Stevie Ray had been sober for three years and was at his peak. When he played that night he had all of us standing there with our jaws dropped."

Above: With Roger Waters of Pink Floyd fame.

Opposite: Clapton playing at the Royal Albert Hall in London in the early nineties.

The resilient guitarist soon bounced back to play twenty-four record-breaking dates at the Royal Albert Hall in February of 1991. Following the satisfying, though exhausting triumph, Clapton flew immediately to New York, eager for a restful interlude with his 4-year-old son, Conor, who was living in Manhattan with his mother. But it was never to be.

In a horrifying accident on 20th March, the boy fell to his death from the window of Clapton's fifty-third floor apartment. In a state of shock and disbelief Eric flew back home to England as the news hit friends and fans worldwide.

Ginger Baker remembers phoning his friend when he learned of the tragedy. "I just told him 'I'm thinking about you, man; keep your chin up.' "

Of those bleak days Clapton said, "I turned to stone. My soul went dead to music. Music couldn't reach me. I tried to go into the studio, but I botched it. This was life before, how can I relate to this?"

Yet, as in times of crisis, like so many times before, the guitar once

Friends for life - Eric Clapton, Ringo Starr and George Harrison join together to celebrate the 30th anniversary of *Blue Suede Shoes* with rockabilly legend, Carl Perkins, in London in 1985.

again became his lifeline. Several months after the accident Eric went off on holiday, taking along a small gut-string guitar, and there the healing began. "I would cry, but I would play. And I started to write little songs. That's how it worked for me."

One of those songs became the cornerstone of Clapton's next project, the scoring for the dark, gritty film, *Rush*, about heroin addiction, a subject he knew well. *Tears in Heaven*, a gentle, wrenching ballad addressed to his departed son and released as a single in 1992, captured the hearts of the music-buying public and became the most requested song of the year.

Clapton found another way to take his mind off his misery, by persuading George Harrison to go on tour for the first time in fifteen years. "He was very nervous, so I said, 'You can have my band, my lights, my sound and we'll go somewhere where people are not too critical and are hungry and enthusiastic, like Japan.' "

Together the pair played six memorable dates in December, 1992 in

Osaka and Tokyo, satisfying fans with an impressive catalog of Harrison hits.

"We still have our little bickers," disclosed Clapton after the historic tour, "but I've known him too long not to still love him."

As 1993 opened, a newly rejuvenated Clapton emerged, ready to don the mantle of fame again. Together with Jack Bruce and Ginger Baker he appeared at LA's Century Plaza Hotel on 12th January for Cream's induction into the Rock'n'Roll Hall of Fame. The performance, marking the band's first public reunion in twenty-five years contained an electrifying set of *Born Under a Bad Sign*, *Sunshine of Your Love* and *Crossroads*.

Baker enthused: "It was like we'd only been apart twenty-five days. And I think the question has been answered. Cream did and will stand the test of time."

In his acceptance speech Clapton had this to say: "Until recently I never believed in this institution. I don't believe in institutions, I suppose. It seemed to me that rock'n'roll should never be respectable. Then a friend of mine, Robbie Robertson, pointed out to me that minor and major miracles take place here. I've been reunited with two people I love very dearly. It's very moving."

Clapton continued his passage to immortality by winning a phenomenal six Grammy Awards the following month. The highlight was winning the Song of the Year honors for *Tears In Heaven*, as well as Album of the Year for the equally acclaimed *Unplugged* album, taken from his acoustic only appearance on an MTV special. The songs were written and selected for Conor.

"Towards the end of his life he had developed such a strong personality that he was able to tell me what I was doing wrong. He was teaching me how to help him grow up and I couldn't believe that. These songs are lyrically about him, to honor his memory."

Unplugged also spawned a languid, melancholy version of *Layla*, which became a hit all over again for an entire new generation, a tribute to the song's strength and timelessness. "I'm incredibly proud of *Layla*," smiles Clapton. "To have ownership of something that powerful is something I'll never be able to get used to. It still knocks me out when I play it. It still has so much bite and soul. I can't imagine not doing *Layla* anywhere."

Today he's graciously taken up the torch of rock's gentle elder statesman. "I don't believe in any kind of excesses any more. I think I'm happy with that. I don't think I'm a workaholic, but I need it in my life quite regularly. And I need to be loved for it. I need to please with what I do and so I will try and remain within the parameters of acceptability."

As Clapton looks back over his shoulder he admits he took a few

Below: With Kathy Lloyd at High Spirits in London in the late eighties.

Above: A typically dapper Clapton with sometime girlfriend, Julia Smith.

wrong turns along the road. "I'm a slow learner and a slow developer. It's taken me a long time. No doubt drink and drugs were instrumental in keeping me from that growth. But it's taken place now. Maybe too late, not too late, I think. But late for sure."

"I've come to terms with my identity now a lot better. In the blues format I can just almost lose consciousness; it's like seeing in the dark. I am and always will be, a blues guitarist."

For more than thirty years the name Eric Clapton has represented virtuoso guitar playing and the very best in popular rhythm and blues. He is still as vital and creative as ever and music fans everywhere can hope for many more great songs, great recordings and great performances.

Opposite: Clapton empties out the till at the Grammy Awards.

ACKNOWLEDGEMENTS

Senior Editors: Brenda Giuliano and Sara Colledge
Executive Researcher: Sesa Nichole Giuliano
Intern: Devin Giuliano

The authors would like to thank the following people for
their kindness in helping to publish this book.

Sriman Jagannatha Dasa Adikari
Dr. Mirza Beg
Stefano Castino
Srimati Vrinda Rani Devi Dasi
Enzo of Valentino
Robin Scot Giuliano
Avalon and India Giuliano
ISKCON
Tim Hailstone
Suneel Jaitly
Jo Messham
Marcus Lecky
His Divine Grace B.H. Mangalniloy Goswami Maharaja
Dr. Michael Klapper
Leaf Leavesley
Donald Lehr
Timothy Leary
Andrew Lownie
Mark Studios, Clarence, New York
David Lloyd McIntyre
His Divine Grace A.C. Bhaktivedanta Swami Prabhupada
Self Realization Institute of America (SRI)
Something Fishy Productions Ltd.
Dave Thompson
Edward Veltman
Dr. Ronald Zucker

PHOTOGRAPHIC ACKNOWLEDGEMENTS

The publishers wish to thank the following organisations for their kind permission to reproduce their
photographs in this publication.

Pictorial Press: cover, half title page, title page, 12, 13, 15, 16 (right), 18, 20, 21, 22, 23 (left),
30, 31, 32, 33, 34, 35, 36, 37, 38, 45, 46, 63, 64, 65, 67, 69, 70, 73, 74-75, 76, 77, 78, 79,
80, 81, 82, 84-85, 86, 87 (left & below), 88 (right), 89, 90, 91, 93, 94, 96.

Rock of Ages Archives: imprint page, 8, 9, 14, 16 (left), 17, 19, 23 (right), 24-25, 26, 27, 28,
29, 39, 40, 41, 43, 44, 47, 54, 59, 62, 71, 72, 87 (top), 88 (left), 95.

Jasmine and Peach Archives: 50, 51, 52, 53, 55, 56, 57.

Photographic Images International: 48, 49, 60, 92